Table of Contents

Welcome

Greetings from the enthralling Loire Valley, a setting for real-life fairy tales! This region, which is located right in the center of France, is well known for its stunning scenery, lovely castles, and renowned vineyards. Get ready to set out on an adventure full of romance, history, and amazing adventures.

Why Loire Valley Should Be on Your Travel Bucket List

If you're unsure of why Loire Valley ought to be at the top of your list of places to visit, allow us to educate you! More than 300 magnificent châteaux can be found in this enchanted place, each one more alluring than the last. As you tour these architectural wonders, from the imposing Château de Chambord to the graceful Château de Chenonceau, you'll be taken back in time.

However, the Loire Valley is unique in many ways than only its castles. The area is renowned for its beautiful vineyards, which yield some of the best wines in the world. So wine lovers, be ready to enjoy the tastes of this heaven for wine enthusiasts.

Essential Tips for Exploring Loire Valley

Now that you're prepared to start your Loire Valley vacation, read on for some vital advice to maximize your trip:

1. Get on two wheels and rent a bicycle. This is one of the best ways to see the Loire Valley. Rent a bike and ride across the picturesque countryside, past vineyards, undulating hills, and quaint villages. It's a pleasant and environmentally responsible way to experience the area's natural splendor.

2. Savor the regional cuisine: Indulge in the culinary treats of the Loire Valley. The area is a food lover's paradise, with everything from exquisite rillettes to delicious goat cheese. For the best dining

experience, try the renowned rillettes, a traditional spread cooked with pork or duck, and sip local wine while you enjoy it.

3. Visit the lesser-known châteaux: Don't pass up the opportunity to see the hidden jewels because the famous châteaux get all the attention. Examine lesser-known châteaux like Château de Brézé or Château de l'Islette to learn about their fascinating histories and stunning architecture. You never know— you might come across a buried gem.

4. Make plans for all four seasons: The Loire Valley is stunning all year long, with each bringing its own distinct charm. Flowers are in bloom in the spring, summer is great for riverside picnics, fall is stunning with colorful foliage, and winter is comfortable. So, whenever you go, there's always something spectacular to discover.

With these crucial hints in your back pocket, get ready to make priceless memories in the captivating Loire Valley. The story can now start!

Getting to Know the Loire Valley

Understanding the Rich History and Cultural Significance

Welcome to the fascinating Loire Valley, where culture and history blend to create an experience that will never be forgotten. As you learn the mysteries of this fascinating area, get ready to set off on a voyage through time.

A long and illustrious history can be found in the Loire Valley. This region has experienced the rise and fall of powerful kingdoms, the production of beautiful architectural wonders, and the beginning of artistic movements that have changed the globe from the medieval to the Renaissance periods.

Exploring the UNESCO World Heritage Sites in Loire Valley

All you history nerds and culture vultures, assemble! The Loire Valley is home to not one but multiple UNESCO World Heritage Sites that will astound you. The historical and architectural significance of the area is attested to by these locations.

Admire the splendor of the Château de Chambord, a magnificent example of Renaissance design. Visit the fascinating Château de Chenonceau, also referred to as the "Ladies' Castle" since it has a long history of being associated with influential ladies. And don't forget to stop by the picturesque village of Amboise, where you'll find the magnificent Château d'Amboise and Leonardo da Vinci's resting place.

The Magnificent Châteaux of Loire Valley

Get ready to be awed by the sheer splendor of the châteaux dotted around the Loire Valley. These architectural marvels are evidence of the opulence and grandeur of the French kings and nobles.

Discover the fairytale-like Château de Villandry, renowned for its stunning gardens that display fascinating geometric patterns. The Château de Blois, which witnessed many historical occurrences and housed multiple French monarchs, has beautiful rooms that will make you feel like royalty.

Every château in the Loire Valley has a distinct narrative that transports you back in time and provides a window into the life of those who once called these beautiful buildings their homes.

So prepare for a unique trip in the Loire Valley by packing your bags and donning your explorer's hat. This area promises an experience that will captivate you thanks to its fascinating history and magnificent châteaux. Watch the Loire Valley's charm come to life before your eyes!

Festivals and Events

Festivals Celebrating Wine and Gastronomy

Those who enjoy wine and cuisine are invited! The Loire Valley is skilled at putting on a feast for your taste sensations. Visit the festivals honoring wine and cuisine to indulge in a feast for the senses. Get ready for a mouthwatering tour of the best delicacies the area has to offer. Let your taste buds dance with joy as you sip on fine wines and enjoy regional specialties. These festivals are an authentic celebration of the region's gastronomic skills, with everything from winery tours to gourmet food markets.

Journées du Patrimoine: Heritage Days Unveiling Hidden Treasures(3rd weekend of september)

The Heritage Days, also known as Journées du Patrimoine, are a time to delve into the mysteries of the past. This occasion gives you privileged access to some of the Loire Valley's best-kept historical secrets. Investigate imposing castles, charming châteaux, and breathtaking museums that are the key to the area's rich legacy. Immerse yourself in the myths and lore that have shaped this extraordinary country. Open the portals to a historical realm, and the past will come to life before your eyes.

Renaissance Festivals: Time Travel to the Past

The lively festivals conducted in the Loire Valley allow visitors to step back in time and experience the magic of the Renaissance era. Get ready to be taken back in time to a period of knights, queens, and artistic genius. Take in the sight of the jousting matches, the magnificent costumes, and the traditional music. Watch as street performers bring historical figures to life while admiring the exquisite craftsmanship. These events offer a once-in-a-lifetime trip through time, whether you're a history buff or just interested in the past.

Prepare to sample the delicacies, find hidden treasures, and travel back in time on an exciting adventure. You will have lifelong memories from the festivals and activities in the Loire Valley. Set aside these dates in your calendars and get ready for a remarkable adventure in this beautiful locale.

Don't miss out on these Loire Valley Renaissance events! From June to September, Chateau du Clos Lucé will host a special exhibition of Leonardo da Vinci's iconic Last Supper tapestry, as well as Renaissance gastronomical evenings. Experience the romance of Valençay Chateau with "Chandelles de la Renaissance," where the chateau and its gardens will illuminate by candlelight from May through October.

Even if the Renaissance isn't your thing, the Loire Valley has a lot to offer. Explore the region's UNESCO attractions, like as the cathedrals of Bourges and Chartres, as well as the Loire Valley itself. During your stay, you will see 6 art and historical cities, 65 museums, and 70 parks and gardens. This charming place has something for everyone!

Exploring the Main Cities of Loire Valley

Tours: The Gateway to Loire Valley

The Historic Old Town of Tours

The old town of Tours' charming cobblestone alleys will transport you back in time. This region is a goldmine of history and culture, with its lovely architecture, bustling marketplaces, and picturesque squares. Take a leisurely stroll and allow history to embrace you.

The Fine Arts Museum of Tours

All lovers of the arts, unite! Don't pass up the chance to lose yourself in the realm of masterpieces at the Tours Fine Arts Museum. Admire the masterful brushwork of famous painters like Monet and Degas, and let their imaginations serve as an inspiration for your own. You'll be in awe of the museum's huge collection and yearn for more.

Gastronomic Delights in Tours' Restaurants

Get ready to embark on a culinary experience in Tours! A wide variety of eateries in this bustling metropolis serve a delicious selection of culinary treats. There is something for every pallet, from classic French cuisine to creative fusion meals. Give yourself a special dining experience and enjoy the Loire Valley's delights.

Getting to Tours, if you decide to start your vacation here:
By Train: The TGV connects Paris to Tours in approximately 35 minutes and Blois in approximately 1 1/2 hours.

By car: it is a 2-1/2-hour drive from Paris to Amboise or Tours.

By Plane: The majority of visitors will arrive in Paris. If you prefer not to fly into Paris, Nantes's airport boasts links to numerous European hubs. It is only two and a half hours by vehicle west of Tours.

Orleans: The City of Joan of Arc

You are invited to go off on a historical adventure unlike any other in Orleans, the charming city famous for its connections to the great Joan of Arc. Discover the amazing story of this fearless warrior, who overcame all odds and made his mark on French history. Explore the same streets where Joan of Arc once walked and feel the spirit of bravery.

The Grandeur of Gothic Orleans Cathedral

Get ready to be astounded by Orleans Cathedral, a magnificent Gothic masterpiece that dominates the city's skyline. Take in its ethereal splendor as the exquisitely crafted stained glass windows cast a rainbow of hues on the revered walls. Allow the sombre ambience of this holy location to take you back in time.

Orleans' Streets

Prepare to appreciate the vibrant energy that pulses through Orleans' streets. Take in the fascinating fusion of old-world architecture and contemporary flare as you stroll along its bustling boulevards. The colorful tapestry of sights, sounds, and tastes in Orleans ranges from cozy cafés to busy marketplaces. Enjoy your senses and savor the joy of living that permeates every nook and cranny.

Don't pass up the chance to learn about Joan of Arc's fascinating life as you go through Orleans, be in awe of the majestic cathedral, and give in to the enticing appeal of the busy streets. Orleans is waiting to dazzle you with its special fusion of the past and present, leaving you with priceless memories to cherish.

Getting to the Loire Valley from Paris, if you decide to start your vacation here:

- Train: The train is the quickest means of transportation, taking passengers from Paris' Austerlitz Station to Orléans in under an hour.

- Car: If you prefer to see more of the Loire Valley, it takes around an hour and a half to drive from Paris. Be prepared, though, to pay high toll road tolls.

Blois: A Renaissance Gem

The Architectural Marvels of Blois Château

The Blois Château's jaw-dropping architectural marvels will wow you! With a stunning fusion of architectural forms, this beautiful Renaissance castle stands proudly. Every nook and cranny conveys a sense of grandeur and wealth, from its exquisite façade to its meticulous details. Explore the opulent apartments that formerly served as kings and queens while channeling your inner history geek. It's nearly required that you take a selfie in front of the castle.

Investigating the Blois Château's Complex Garden

It's time to lose yourself in the magical embrace of the Blois Château Garden after you've had your fill of architectural magnificence. A wonderful retreat from the rush of modern life is provided by this painstakingly created oasis. Enjoy a leisurely stroll down the well-kept sidewalks that are bordered by colorful flowers and neatly trimmed hedges. Let the peace wash over you as you take a moment to inhale the sweet air. This garden is a must-see whether you enjoy the outdoors or are just looking for a tranquil getaway.

Blois's Charming Old Town Revealed

As you stroll around the Old Town of Blois, you'll experience a time travel. Get lost in the deep history that permeates every cobblestone and century-old structure. Discover hidden gems at every turn as you meander through the little passageways. Discover one-of-a-kind finds and keepsakes to remember your trip by perusing the neighborhood stores and boutiques. Don't forget to sample the regional cuisine at one of the charming cafés or restaurants, where you may appreciate authentic treats that will send your taste buds into a frenzy.

Therefore, Blois awaits with its Renaissance wonders, lovely gardens, and an enthralling Old Town, dear traveler. Prepare to be transported to a bygone period where history and beauty meet in the Loire Valley's center.

Châteaux-Hopping in Loire Valley

Welcome to the country of fabled forts and beautiful scenery! Get ready to be mesmerized as we go across the Loire Valley's Châteaux on an incredible tour. Get ready for an unforgettable château-hopping experience where dreams come true and history comes to life.

Château de Chambord: A Masterpiece of French Renaissance

The Grandeur of Château de Chambord

When you first see the imposing Château de Chambord, you ready to have your breath stolen away. You will be in awe of this architectural marvel with its beautiful fusion of French Renaissance and classical Italian styles. It is a large, imposing structure that displays its complex decorations and tall spires. It was constructed as a hunting lodge for King Francis I.

As you explore the huge chambers filled with complex tapestries, priceless paintings, and opulent furnishings suitable for royalty, you'll be transported into a world of splendor. As a royal visitor, picture yourself taking in the splendor of this amazing work of art.

French Gardens and the Wide Grounds

A wide area of lush vegetation and well planned gardens can be found beyond the majestic façade. Take in the peace of the French gardens as you meander along the immaculately trimmed paths. Be in awe of the perfect designs of the flowerbeds, the heavenly scents of the blossoms, and the serene ponds that reflect the beauty above.

Spend a minute unwinding under a shady tree, letting the breeze carry your cares away. The gardens of the Château de Chambord are a haven of calm that beckons you to commune with nature and savor life's little joys.

A Rooftop Ascent for Panoramic Views

As you ascend to the Château de Chambord's rooftop, get ready for an amazing display of splendor. Here, you may experience the Loire Valley's real splendor. Take in the expansive, eye-catching views of the surrounding countryside. You won't soon forget the stunning postcard-like landscape of the rolling hills, meandering rivers, and quaint villages.

Allow the splendor of the surroundings to envelop your senses as you stand atop this work of art. The rooftop of the Château de Chambord offers the ideal vantage point to observe the balance between created wonders and the natural world.

Prepare to be amazed by the elegance and majesty of Château de Chambord. This is a time-defying encounter where history whispers in your ear and beauty twirls before your very eyes. This magnificent example of French Renaissance architecture is a great place to start your château-hopping tour of the Loire Valley.

Château de Chenonceau: The Iconic Bridge Château

Crossing the Spectacular Arched Bridge of Chenonceau

As you travel through the spectacular arched bridge of Château de Chenonceau, get ready for an unforgettable experience. This renowned building spans the glistening Cher River and is a work of beauty, not just any old bridge. Be prepared to be taken to a time of wealth and grandeur as soon as you set foot on this work of art.

The bridge, which connects the château's two sides, stands erect like a regal entrance to the realm of magic that dwells there. It is understandable why the Chenonceau bridge has developed into one of the Loire Valley's most identifiable sights with its flowing arches and magnificent design. Enjoy the scenery for a while, take some breath-taking photos, and

then let the bridge lure you on to your next
adventure.

History and Elegance of the Château

When you arrive at Château de Chenonceau
after crossing the bridge, get ready to be
amazed by its unmistakable elegance and
extensive past. Numerous historical luminaries
have visited this architectural marvel, which
has also endured the test of time and seen
royal intrigues.

As soon as you enter the vast halls, you'll be
whisked away to a time when nobles ruled
supreme. Admire the magnificent furnishings,
elaborate tapestries, and exquisite artwork that
adorn the chambers, each of which tells a
distinct tale of the château's past. Learn about
the influential ladies, such as Diane of Poitiers
and Catherine de' Medici, who left their stamp
on Chenonceau and feel their presence
permeate the building.

Imagine the opulent parties and top-secret
meetings that once occurred within these walls

as you explore the different chambers. As you take in the myths and tales that have built this amazing site, you will feel the weight of history. Whatever your interest in history, Château de Chenonceau is certain to leave a lasting impression on your soul.

Beautiful Parkland and Gardens

Beyond the imposing château, you can explore the expansive landscape's charming gardens and parkland at your leisure. Take a leisurely stroll around the immaculately maintained gardens, where colorful flowers explode with color and aromas fill the air. Let your imagination soar in this natural wonderland as you become lost in the maze-like hedges.

Explore the pathways lined with trees and look for tucked-away nooks and crannies that reveal stunning views and serene areas for reflection. The grounds at Château de Chenonceau have been meticulously planned to complement the surrounding landscape and produce a picture-perfect scene that seems to have come right out of a fairy tale.

Enjoy the peace and tranquility of this ideal sanctuary while being surrounded by the beauty of nature. The gardens and parkland of Chenonceau provide a haven of calm, whether you're trying to achieve inner peace or are just trying to get away from the chaos of daily life.

You'll take with you memories of a remarkable voyage through history, elegance, and natural grandeur as the sun sets on your adventure at Château de Chenonceau. So go ahead and start your château-hopping adventure in the Loire Valley and allow the beauty of Château de Chenonceau to enchant you.

Château d'Amboise: Royal Residence with Leonardo da Vinci Connection

Visit the Former Royal Residence of Château d'Amboise

Embark on a voyage to the majestic Château d'Amboise and enter a realm of regal beauty. This renowned château, located along the scenic Loire River, emits an unmistakable charm that will take you back in time to the splendor of the Renaissance.

You'll be enthralled by the architectural splendor and extensive history of this magnificent home as you stroll through its halls. Marvel at the elaborate Gothic façade's decorations and let your imagination soar as you imagine the opulent celebrations that previously took place inside these very walls.

Take a look at Leonardo da Vinci's last resting place.

Get ready to be amazed as you learn about the fascinating relationship between Château d'Amboise and the brilliant brain, Leonardo da Vinci. As he spent his final years in the nearby town of Amboise, the genius himself used this remarkable château as a final haven.

Visit Leonardo da Vinci's grave, which is located inside the Saint-Hubert Chapel, to learn more about his life and accomplishments. This holy place honors the remarkable mind behind the ground-breaking innovations and works of art that changed the globe for all time.

Views from the Château's Terrace that Will Astound You

As you climb to the terrace of the Château d'Amboise, you may expect to be astounded by the breathtaking views of the Loire Valley that greet you. From this unique vantage point, the meandering river, luscious vineyards, and rolling hills form a breathtaking visual symphony that will take your breath away.

Take a moment to savor the breathtaking natural beauty that is all around you and to reflect on how magnificent your surroundings truly are. Allow a sensation of peace to wash over you as the soft air caresses your face as you take in the unmatched view.

Be careful to record this enchanted moment with your camera as the sun sends its golden rays across the landscape because moments like these should be treasured forever.

A magnificent experience that combines history, art, and natural beauty is provided by Château d'Amboise. This château provides an amazing trip back in time, complete with the magnificent royal home and Leonardo da Vinci's final resting place. Don't forget to take in the breathtaking views from the terrace, where the Loire Valley's splendor is revealed to you. Your imagination will be sparked and your heart will be forever changed when you visit Château d'Amboise. Grab your sense of wonder and go château-hopping in the captivating Loire Valley on an extraordinary journey!

To Château hop with ease, take either a taxi or drive with your rented car
The cost is estimated by Taxi is between $130 and $160.
The cost is estimated by drive is between $10 and $15.

Indulging in Loire Valley's Culinary Delights

1. Wine Tasting in Loire Valley's Vineyards

The Loire Valley is the pinnacle of wine-fueled enjoyment when it comes to tasting wine. Get ready for an incredible voyage through vineyards that will have you doing the grapevine dance as your taste senses are in for a treat! You will be mesmerized by the perfume of high-quality wines the instant you step foot in this area.

Try Some of the Known White Wines of the Loire Valley

White wines from the Loire Valley are renowned for being crisp and delicate and will make your palate dance with delight. You'll be taken to a world of subtle flavors and fruity overtones with each sip. Enjoy the well-known Sancerre, a lively white wine that captures the spirit of the Loire Valley. You'll want more because of the tartness and citrus undertones in it. Don't pass up the delicious Vouvray Chenin Blanc, a Chenin Blanc that will enchant your senses with its honeyed scents and creamy texture. Each vineyard has its own special charm, and you'll find a wide variety of white wine kinds that will delight your palate and put you in a blissful state of vino.

Find information about the Wine Routes and Cellars.

Follow the twisting roads that take you through the Loire Valley's wine pathways to properly begin a wine trip. You'll get to see the craftsmanship of winemaking up close as you stroll through lovely vineyards. Experience the earthy link to the origins of wine making by taking a journey through the landscapes covered in vines. Discover the winemakers' secrets as you explore their basements, where barrels and bottles are waiting patiently for their chance to shine. You'll see the love and commitment that go into creating these exceptional wines with each step.

Wine and Local Cheese and Cuisine Matching

Without the ideal food pairing, what good is a great wine? The Loire Valley can handle it! As you sample the local cheese and cuisine with your preferred wines, indulge in the culinary art of food matching. Let the tastes blend together to create a mouth-watering symphony of flavor on your palette. Try the delicious Crottin de Chavignol, a creamy goat cheese that is the perfect accompaniment to a glass of Sancerre. For the most daring foodies out there, try rillettes and taste this hearty, flavorful dish with a glass of full-bodied Chinon. You're in for an unparalleled culinary excursion, and the choices are unlimited.

Wine tasting is more than simply a pastime in the Loire Valley; it's a way of life. So come on over, raise a glass, and savor the flavors and scents that make up this magical region. Allow the Loire Valley's vineyards and wines to transport you on a memorable journey that will leave you with memories and a renewed respect for the craft of winemaking. Cheers to a unique experience that will make you want more!

Explore the Maisons du vins in Nantes, Angers, Saumur, and Tours, offering a wide selection of over seventy hand-picked wines from the Loire

Valley's forty appellations. Enjoy tastings with no pressure to purchase. Additionally, visit the impressive 'Cave de Producteurs' at Vouvray and Montlouis-sur-Loire, or opt for a unique experience at an independent producer's tasting room on their property.

Gastronomic Experiences in Loire Valley

Delight in Traditional Loire Valley Cuisine

The Loire Valley doesn't let you down when it comes to traditional food. In order to take you to a world of culinary delight, get ready for your taste buds to embark on a delectable voyage via centuries-old recipes and flavors. This area offers a beautiful tapestry of flavours, from simple country dinners to sumptuous delicacies fit for royalty.

The renowned rillettes are without a doubt one of the culinary highlights of the Loire Valley. Imagine delicious beef in tender shreds that have been perfectly cooked and seasoned over a long period of time to create a mouthwatering flavor. Rillettes, whether they are made of pork, duck, or even fish, are the height of decadence. You will experience gourmet bliss if you spread them on a crisp baguette.

There's still more, though! Delicious goat cheese, or chèvre as it's known locally, may also be found in the Loire Valley. This creamy and tangy treat comes in a variety of sizes and shapes, and each one has a distinctive flavor. Enjoy a straightforward goat cheese salad or try the regional delicacy Sainte-Maure-de-Touraine, a cylindrical cheese rolled in ash and straw. Your taste buds will tingle with delight with every bite.

Let's now discuss the main attraction, the Loire Valley wines. The vineyards in this area are world-renowned, and a wide variety of wines are made there. Drink some crisp, hydrating Sancerre or explore the world of bubbly treats with a bottle of Vouvray. The vineyards of the Loire Valley offer a sensory experience that will leave you wanting more, whether you're a wine specialist or a casual fan.

Check out regional markets and food festivals.

Make sure to stop by one of the many regional markets and food festivals to fully experience the Loire Valley's thriving culinary culture. These hopping centers of culinary delights provide a feast for the senses and an opportunity to meet passionate regional producers.

Wander around the lively market stalls that are bursting at the seams with a variety of fresh fruits, vegetables, artisanal cheeses, and fragrant herbs. Select the best components for your upcoming culinary journey while exchanging pleasantries with the sellers. Allow the dazzling hues and alluring fragrances to lead you to undiscovered ingredients that will take your cooking to a new level.

Don't miss the vibrant culinary festivals that highlight the area's gastronomy if you decide to visit during the summer. Enjoy delectable street food while taking in the lively ambiance created by live music and the contagious excitement in the air. These events, which range from the Fête de la Gastronomie to the Festivini wine festival, open doors to a world of delectable foods and priceless memories.

Try Local Specialties and Delights

Regional specialties and delights that will leave you wanting more dot the culinary landscape of the Loire Valley. Set out on a culinary experience that highlights the distinctive flavors of the area after settling up at a quaint country inn or comfortable café.

Start with "Tarte Tatin," a traditional meal that is considered to be the symbol of the Loire Valley. The skill of French pastry is truly demonstrated in this decadent caramelized upside-down apple tart. Each bite shows a perfectly balanced mixture of sweet and sour aromas that are all encased in a flaky, buttery crust. You should treat yourself to this dessert, we promise.

For the carnivores among you, be sure to enjoy a platter of "Rillauds." Slow cooking results in meltingly delicate, succulent slices of pork belly. The outcome is a dish that is savory and rich, showcasing the best of the Loire Valley's culinary customs.

Don't forget to savor the area's delicious treats as well. The Loire Valley's dessert scene is nothing short of extraordinary, with exquisite "Poires Tapées" (pressed pears) and delicate "Macarons de Cormery" made with almonds. Treat your taste senses to the symphony of tastes by indulging in these tiny pieces of bliss.

Food lovers looking for a unique gastronomic experience will find paradise in the Loire Valley. Enjoy regional specialties and delicacies that will make a lasting impression, explore the bustling markets and culinary festivals, and indulge in traditional cuisine. Prepare yourself for a gastronomic adventure that will win your heart and satiate your appetites like never before. Good food!

Outdoor Adventures in Loire Valley

Prepare Yourself for Thrills and Spills!

The Loire Valley is not simply known for its beautiful scenery and ancient castles; it is also a haven for thrill seekers. Put your seatbelts on, fasten your helmet, and get ready for an exhilarating ride through nature. The Loire Valley offers a variety of thrilling sports that will leave you gasping for air and wishing there were more, from biking along the Loire River to soaring over the breathtaking scenery in a hot air balloon. Let's plunge into the thrilling adventures that are in store!

Cycling Along the Loire River

Ride a Bike to Paradise!

1. Take a bike ride along the Loire à Vélo route.

All cycling enthusiasts, assemble! The Loire à Vélo is one of the world's most amazing bicycle routes, and it is located in the Loire Valley. This fascinating road, which spans more than 800 kilometers, winds past picturesque villages, breathtaking landscape, and, of course, spectacular châteaux. As you peddle your way past vineyards, sunflower fields, and the serene banks of the Loire River, immerse yourself in the alluring surroundings. This two-wheeled journey is ideal for experienced cyclists as well as leisure riders, with clearly delineated trails and rental services available.

2. Appreciate Riverside Views and Beautiful Bike Paths

Prepare to be astounded by the breathtaking views along the Loire River. A cool wind will caress your face as you pedal around the region's well-maintained bike trails on your trusted bicycle. Beautiful scenery appears before your eyes, with a peaceful river on one side and luscious vineyards on the other. Take a picnic lunch next to the water or cool yourself in the Loire's mild currents. This bike adventure guarantees a fantastic blend of the outdoors, culture, and pure adrenaline.

3. Travel by bicycle through the villages and castles

Transform your four wheels into two and set out on a whimsical tour through the charming villages and fairytale-like châteaux of the Loire Valley. You'll experience a character out of a storybook as you pedal through the quaint streets. Discover undiscovered treasures, happen across local markets stocked to the brim with mouthwatering goodies, and take in the enchanting ambiance that makes this area very special. Your oyster is the Loire Valley, and cycling is the key to discovering all of its numerous beauties.

Hot Air Balloon Rides over Loire Valley

Aerial Style: Take to the Skies!

1. Take a Bird's-Eye View of the Loire Valley's Stunning Landscape

There is no better way to enhance your Loire Valley experience than from a regal hot air balloon, which will lift you majestically above the landscape. As you soar into the skies and disappear below, the world below will appear as a colorful mosaic, leaving you in amazement. As far as the eye can see, there is a patchwork of vineyards, undulating hills, and charming châteaux. You will be in awe of the spectacular beauty of the area thanks to this bird's-eye view, which will give you a fresh viewpoint.

2. Fly Over Chateaux and Vineyards

As you soar over the most famous sites in the Loire Valley, get ready to have your senses tantalized. From the exquisite turrets of Château de Chambord to the sumptuous gardens of Villandry, each château presents its beauty from a completely different viewpoint. Observe winegrowers carefully tending to their priceless grapes as you soar over vast vineyards and take in the fascinating patterns of the ground below. A lifetime of memories will be made thanks to this once-in-a-lifetime event.

Third, Soar Above the Loire Valley

Leave your worries behind as you enter the enchanted realm of hot air ballooning. Embraced by a sense of peace and amazement, drift gently across the sky. As your skilled pilot navigates the winds, the only sound that occasionally breaks the silence is the whooshing of the burner. Join a centuries-old custom that captivates the imagination like nothing else and feel the magic in the air. A hot air balloon flight in the Loire Valley will take you to a world of unmatched enchantment, whether you're commemorating a particular occasion or just looking for a moment of pure happiness. Book a tour ride in either Viator.com or Tripadvisor.com, prices vary with time we advise that you compare prices before book.

Prepare yourself for adventure.

Family-Friendly Activities

In the alluring Loire Valley, are there any thrilling excursions that the whole family can partake in? You've found it! With a list of fun family activities, we've got you covered. These activities will make your kids grin from ear to ear and leave everyone with priceless memories. Prepare yourself for a voyage full of wonder and thrill!

1. Zooparc de Beauval: A World-Class Zoo Adventure

Prepare to roar with delight at the Zooparc de Beauval, a wonderful jewel tucked away in the Loire Valley. For animal lovers of all ages, this top-notch zoo is a joy. As you come in contact with over 10,000 animals, including some of the rarest and most exotic species on the earth, get ready to be in wonder.

This zoo has everything, from regal elephants to comical penguins, gorgeous giraffes to mischievous monkeys. The animals at the Zooparc de Beauval are content and healthy because their meticulously created habitats closely resemble those in which they were born. A truly amazing encounter will result from your opportunity to explore their magnificence up close and personal.

But the excitement doesn't end there! Prepare yourself for daily performances by acrobatic dolphins, endearing sea lions, and even stunning bird displays. These outstanding performances will enthrall not only you but even your children.

2. Mini-Châteaux Park(Amboise): Bringing Fairytales to Life for Children

At Mini-Châteaux Park, you may enter a world straight out of a fairy tale. For both kids and adults, this beautiful park is a veritable fantasy. Imagine strolling through a minutely detailed tiny community where each and every aspect has been painstakingly replicated to highlight the region's most renowned castles and châteaux.

As they explore this fascinating world and feel like giants among these miniature wonders, watch your children's eyes light up with excitement. They will get the chance to explore the architectural wonders that characterize the Loire Valley, from the magnificence of Château de Chambord to the grace of Château de Chenonceau.

But it goes beyond just being a visual wonder. Children can learn about the background and lore of these spectacular structures through interactive exhibits at Mini-Châteaux Park. The opportunity to travel through time and let their imaginations run wild make it more than just a park.

3. Canoeing on the Loire River Is Safe and Fun for Everyone

Are you looking for an outdoor experience that combines fun, relaxation, and a touch of the outdoors while you're in Orleans? For a canoeing adventure on the Loire River, grab your paddles and go out. Families wanting a special time together in the midst of the area's breathtaking scenery should engage in this activity.

Canoeing on the Loire River is a fun and safe activity for people of all ages, experienced paddlers as well as total beginners. Enjoy the stunning sights of the charming villages and old castles that dot the riverbanks as you float over the calm currents amidst the lush foliage.

Find a quiet area by the river, pack a picnic, and relax while savoring some delectable snacks and taking in the peace and quiet of nature. In addition to being a river, the Loire River serves as a playground for families looking for both adventure and peace.

Gather your loved ones, don your hats of exploration, and let the Loire Valley work its magic. You'll undoubtedly make lifelong memories with the help of these family-friendly activities. Prepare yourself for a journey full of delight, amazement, and laughter!

Leisure and Relaxation

The lovely Loire Valley is where you can unwind and enjoy yourself! Get ready for a remarkable adventure filled with calm, pristine beauty, and indulgent treatment. The most enjoyable ways to relax and rejuvenate your soul in the midst of this breathtaking area are revealed in this part.

1. Loire River Cruises: A Calm Tour of the Valley

Hallo, comrades in the road! Get ready to go on an enchanted journey down the tranquil Loire River. Sit back and relax as one of the picturesque river boats takes you through the heart of the valley. Enjoy the stunning vistas that have long served as an inspiration to painters and authors as you cruise by.

Feel your tension evaporate as you float by verdant vineyards, historic castles, and charming towns scattered along the riverbanks. Make your pals back home envious by taking some images that will inspire jealousy. As you salute your memorable journey, don't forget to raise a glass of the best local wine!

2. Picnicking in the Loire Countryside: Joy in the Natural World

Want to spend some time in nature? For a wonderful encounter with Mother Nature, gather your picnic supplies and travel to the Loire countryside. The valley has numerous beautiful picnic areas, each one more alluring than the last.

You can find a quaint spot among the vineyards, beneath the shady elms, or next to the peaceful streams. Set up your blanket for a picnic and indulge in the mouthwatering regional specialties that will have your taste buds dancing with delight.

Take a time to appreciate the little things that make life genuinely wonderful as you breathe in the fresh air and take in the natural beauty.

Picnicking in the Loire countryside with loved ones, family, or friends will be an event you'll never forget.

3. Pamper Yourself in Peaceful Environments at Spa Retreats

Enjoy a lavish spa vacation in the country of kings and queens and treat yourself like royalty. Your well-deserved pampering session will provide the ideal environment thanks to the calm Loire Valley. Enjoy a selection of spa services that will melt your tension away, leaving you feeling revitalized and ready to take on the world.

Choose from a variety of top-notch spa resorts that may satisfy any need. Take in the calming scents of essential oils while receiving a peaceful massage. Invigorate your body and soul by diving into mineral-rich thermal waters. Let knowledgeable therapists do their magic and carry you to a place of complete tranquility.

After a spa day, you'll feel as though you're walking on air and be eager to take advantage of all the magical things the Loire Valley has to offer.

Please keep in mind that the Loire Valley is a luxurious getaway from the daily rat race rather than just a tourist attraction. So, take a river cruise, enjoy a picnic in the great outdoors, and succumb to the temptation of spa retreats. You'll be grateful to your soul for it. Enjoy your time off and downtime in the Loire Valley!

Hidden Gems and Off-the-Beaten-Path

Adventurers, hold on to your hats! We're going to go on an exciting tour of the Loire Valley's best-kept secrets, the undiscovered wonders and off-the-beaten-path gems that will make you feel as though you've stumbled into a treasure trove of magic and mystery!

Tales of Castles and Writers in The Mystery of Montsoreau

Montsoreau is a double dose of magic, so pay attention, history enthusiasts and bookworms! This lovely town, tucked away along the winding Loire River, has two reasons to make you shiver.

Let's talk about castles first. The gorgeous ancient castle in Montsoreau is like something out of a fairy tale. Think of imposing stone walls, a friendly drawbridge that formerly deterred attackers but now is warmly welcoming, and a stunning view of the river from the top. It is a palace that will make you fantasize about knights, princesses, and perilous adventures!

There's still more, though! There is another literary trick under Montsoreau's sleeve. Are you familiar with Alexandre Dumas, the author of "The Three Musketeers" and "The Count of Monte Cristo"? Rumor has it that Montsoreau was the source of inspiration for one of his works. Writers, get ready to have your inspirations sparked as you stroll through the same winding alleyways and majestic scenery that once inspired Dumas.

There are two basic ways to go to Saumur:

1. By air: The closest airports are Tours and Angers, both about 70-80 kilometers apart. These airports provide car rentals and train connections to Saumur.

2. By train: If you do not intend to rent a car, traveling the train is an excellent option. From Paris, you can travel directly to Saumur via Tours (2 hours with a decent connection) or Angers (2.5 hours). GoEuro is suggested for precise scheduling and advance reservations. You may buy train tickets in the station from

machines that provide an English language option, so language will not be an issue.

There are a number of ways to travel to Montsoreau. If you arrive by train, the most convenient but relatively expensive option (about €25) is to take a taxi. trips go from Saumur to Montsoreau, however the schedule is irregular, with more than an hour between trips during the day. Another option for increased mobility is to rent a car in Saumur.

Lavardin: A Stunning Medieval Village

Fairy tales aren't simply for bedtime stories, contrary to what you might believe. Lavardin is an actualized version of a live, breathing fairy tale that has emerged from the pages. This idyllic medieval village, hidden on a mountaintop, is the stuff of legends.

You'll have the impression that you've entered a magical gateway as you get closer to Lavardin. Each of the half-timbered homes is surrounded by colorful flowers that appear to be waving a friendly welcome as cobblestone streets wind through the maze of them. The quaintness and peace that permeate this medieval wonderland's every nook and cranny cannot not but charm you.

Lavardin's magnificent Romanesque church, a work of art that stands erect among the community's natural splendor, is the focal point of its entrancing allure. To get a breathtaking view of the surrounding landscape, hike up to the medieval castle remains if you feel like it. That sight will undoubtedly stay in your mind forever!

Château de Brézé: Elegance and Underground Labyrinths

The Loire Valley is full of magnificent castles, but have you ever wondered what lies beneath one of them? The Château de Brézé is a hidden jewel that goes beyond simple aesthetic appeal, so get ready to have your mind blown!

A vast network of tunnels and labyrinths are hidden beneath this exquisite Renaissance château, which is a fascinating secret. Take a deep breath and fall into a fascinating world that was once the noble dwellers' haven and wine cellar. You'll experience goosebumps on this historical adventure!

The Château de Brézé rises tall and high above the ground, with graceful façade, rich gardens, and an undeniable air of grandeur. Take a look around its lavish rooms, see the ornate tapestries, and picture yourself living the life of a real French nobleman.

Intrepid travelers, that's all there is to it! Adventurers like you are yearning to find the Loire Valley's secret treasures and off-the-beaten-path wonders. Prepare to explore the enigmas of Montsoreau, stroll through the idyllic town of Lavardin, and explore the Château de Brézé's subterranean labyrinths. In

a world where magic and elegance converge,
it's time to make enduring memories!

Accommodation

In Tours

BUDGET: Hilton Garden Inn Tours Centre, France is a 4-star hotel in Tours, France, with an excellent rating of 8.6 based on 2009 reviews. There is a fitness center, a shared lounge, a patio, and a restaurant at the hotel. Guests may take advantage of free WiFi, room service, and a 24-hour front desk. The air-conditioned rooms have a desk, kettle, fridge, safety deposit box, flat-screen TV, and private bathroom with a shower. Each morning, an American breakfast is offered. The hotel's central position provides easy access to the city's attractions and areas of interest, including the Hotel Goüin Museum, the Basilica of Saint Martin, the Vinci International Congress Center, and the Tours Train Station. Tours Val de Loire Airport is 6 kilometers away.

MID-RANGE: Château Belmont Tours by The Crest Collection is a 4-star hotel located in a tranquil 2.5-hectare park in Tours city center, France. The hotel provides modern air-conditioned guest rooms in the rebuilt 17th-century castle or in the home, each with facilities such as a TV, minibar, and free WiFi. Guests can relax in the heated swimming pool, steam room, sauna, and exercise area. The hotel's restaurant and bar serve a breakfast buffet and traditional French cuisine. The hotel also has a relaxing spa area. The park, which is shared with a high-end housing for independent seniors, includes listed trees and an ornamental pond. On-site bicycle rental is offered, and the hotel is ideally positioned 5.8 kilometers from the Saint-Pierre-des-Corps TGV train station.

LUXURY: Les Trésorières is a 5-star hotel in the heart of Tours, France. It has a high rating of 9.2 based on 174 reviews and has a fitness center, terrace, and bar. The hotel offers air-conditioned rooms with modern amenities such as a desk, coffee machine, minibar, and flat-screen TV. Each morning, guests can enjoy complimentary WiFi and a continental breakfast. In addition, the hotel has an indoor pool, sauna, and hammam for leisure. The Basilica of Saint Martin and Hotel Goüin Museum are also within walking distance, as are the Vinci International Congress Center and Tours Train Station. The nearest airport is Tours

Val de Loire Airport, which is 6 kilometers away from the hotel.

In Orleans

BUDGET: The Ibis budget Orléans Sud Comet in Orléans offers modern rooms with complimentary Wi-Fi and private parking. Guests may enjoy a buffet breakfast, and the hotel is close to restaurants and attractions such as Sainte-Croix Cathedral and the Loire River. The hotel is also close to leading cosmetic brand laboratories and recreational facilities such as a shopping center, go-karts, and a bowling alley. There are family rooms, non-smoking rooms, and facilities for disabled people among the amenities.

MID-RANGE: This modern hotel, located along the Loire River and close to the city center, offers pleasant rooms with attached bathrooms, a TV, and a 24-hour front desk. Every morning, guests may enjoy a full buffet breakfast, and there is a nice lounge bar with comfortable seating. The hotel is conveniently positioned near attractions such as the Museum of Fine Arts and Sainte-Croix Cathedral. It is easily accessible through the A10 highway, and on-site public parking is available. The hotel is popular with couples and has many repeat visitors.

LUXURY: The Empreinte Hotel & Spa is a 4-star boutique hotel on the banks of the Loire River. The hotel has several spa facilities, a bar, and a meeting room. Guests can access complimentary WiFi throughout the resort. Each room has a private bathroom with either a bathtub or a walk-in shower, as well as a mini-bar and a welcome tray. The Junior Suites and Suites have river views and balneotherapy baths. A buffet breakfast with sweet and savory foods, as well as local goods, is offered daily in the breakfast room, and guests can also select for in-room breakfast for an extra fee. The sauna, steam room, and herbal tea room are all complimentary at the Empreinte Hotel & Spa. Guests praise the hotel's location, which is close to major attractions such as the Historical and Archaeological Museum of Orleans, Cathedrale Ste-Croix, and Orléans Botanical Garden. Couples particularly like the hotel's location, giving it a grade of 9.3 for a two-person trip.

In Blois

BUDGET: Cit'Hotel Logis Louise de Savoie is a beautiful hotel on the banks of the Loire River, within a 5-minute walk from the Château de Blois. The hotel has individually decorated rooms with free Wi-Fi, a bar, and facilities such as a telephone and flat-screen TV in each room. Guests can enjoy a buffet breakfast with a range of alternatives, and adjacent restaurants are accessible for supper. For your convenience, the hotel provides complimentary luggage storage as well as a bicycle shed. Its strategic location offers quick access to notable castles such as Château de Chambord and Château de Cheverny. Blois Train Station is also nearby, with shuttle buses to the castles. Couples find the location extremely enticing, earning it a high ranking for a romantic holiday.

MID-RANGE: The Ibis Blois Centre Château is a centrally located hotel in Blois with complimentary Wi-Fi and a 24-hour bar. The air-conditioned rooms include a flat-screen TV, a desk, and a private bathroom with a shower and a hairdryer. The hotel has a breakfast buffet with a variety of foods. It is close to the Château de Blois and the Museum of Fine Arts. The lift and the adjoining A10 highway are also convenient for guests. The hotel has garnered great feedback for its location, making it a popular choice for couples.

LUXURY: Mercure Blois Centre is a well-located hotel on Quai Saint Jean, about 500 meters from Blois city center. Guests get free access to the fitness center and wellness area, which includes an indoor heated pool, sauna, steam room, and hot tub. The motel has free WiFi throughout. The air-conditioned rooms include modern facilities such as a flat-screen TV, Wi-Fi access, and a courtesy tray with tea and coffee. The hotel has a restaurant, "Le Quai," that serves regional cuisine produced from seasonal ingredients, as well as a bar, "Wine Not?" that serves drinks and cocktails. A business center, meeting rooms, free bicycle storage, and safe parking are also available. Blois Chateau is a quick 20-minute walk away, and Cheverny and Chambord Castles are both within a 20-minute drive. Couples particularly love the hotel's location.

Planning Your Visit to Loire Valley

Best Time to Visit Loire Valley

Oh my goodness, the Loire Valley! This magical location is a treat all year long, but certain seasons are truly appropriate for a king or queen. Let me tell you when it's ideal to visit this country of fairy tales.

1. Spring (April to May): Spring is a dream come true with its picture-perfect blossoms and vivid scenery. You'll feel as though you've walked into a painting as the castles come to life among the sea of vibrant flowers. You'll get a head start before the tourist crowds arrive because the weather is moderate and pleasant.

2. Summer (June–August): Enjoy long, sunny days, comfortable temperatures, and a lively atmosphere in the Loire Valley summer. The weather is ideal for taking in the beauty of nature, strolling through lush gardens, and enjoying picnics by the river. Simply plan for more

people and think about making reservations for lodging and attractions in advance.

3. Autumn (September to October): The Loire Valley is transformed into a dazzling kaleidoscope of colors as the leaves begin to change. The region has continued to experience favorable weather, and the wine harvest season adds a special quality. There will be less noise, giving you more time to leisurely stroll through the picturesque towns and vineyards.

4. Winter (November–March): Ah, the Loire Valley in the wintertime! Despite the cold, the area nevertheless has a way of charming tourists. Cozy fireside evenings with a drink of local wine are absolutely delicious, and the castles decorated with dazzling lights create a magical atmosphere. You'll also get a chance to get some fantastic lodging discounts.

Options for Lodging in the Loire Valley

After a day of exploring castles and vineyards, you're looking for somewhere to lay your weary head down. Do not be alarmed, dear tourist; the Loire Valley offers lodging options to meet every preference and price range. You'll discover the ideal location to fulfill your fantasies, from opulent châteaux to quaint guesthouses.

1. Château Hotels: Live like a king or queen by booking a room at one of the exquisite château hotels dispersed around the area. These grand estates have been converted into opulent lodgings with elegant apartments, delectable dining options, and first-rate service. It provides an opportunity to enjoy contemporary amenities while taking in the splendour of the past.

2. Boutique Hotels: If you want a more individualized and private experience, stay at a boutique hotel in the Loire Valley. These quaint places are full of personality and style,

frequently hidden away in lovely villages or surrounded by vineyards. Get ready to be caressed and mesmerized by their distinct appeal.

Want a home away from home? Consider self-catering cottages. Think about leasing a self-contained home or apartment in the Loire Valley. The opportunity to prepare your own meals, unwind in your own space, and fully immerse yourself in the local way of life are all provided by these inviting retreats. It's ideal for groups of people or those looking for a more independent vacation experience.

Resources at the end of this book include a list of websites where you can find numerous deals.

Getting Around the Loire Valley by Transportation

It's simple to go around the Loire Valley, my wanderlust-filled friend. Here are some transportation choices to get you to the magnificent sights and beyond:

1. Car Rental: With a car rental, you may travel at your own speed while discovering the Loire Valley. Highways throughout the area make it simple to get from one picturesque village to another. A car also makes it possible to find things off the usual road and find hidden jewels as you travel.

2. Trains: Traveling between important cities and towns in the Loire Valley is quick and easy thanks to the French train system. Settle back as you ride a train through the beautiful countryside. Since train stations are frequently found in the middle of cities, getting where you want to go is usually simple.

3. Bicycles: What a perfect pairing the Loire Valley and bicycles are! An ideal experience is pedaling through the vineyards and alongside the Loire River. Bike rentals are available in many towns, and designated cycling lanes take you through the region's breathtaking scenery. This is a wonderful opportunity to enjoy the

fresh air and take your time to appreciate the beauty all around you.

4. Guided Tours: If you'd like an adventure without hassles, think about going on one. While offering interesting anecdotes and insights about the area, knowledgeable guides will handle all the logistics. These escorted excursions make sure you don't miss a beat whether you choose a castle tour, a wine tasting excursion, or a leisurely river cruise. Websites like getyourguide.com offer tour guides for hire. In the Resources section, there is further information on this.

You are now prepared to start off on a voyage across the enchanted Loire Valley, dear traveler, equipped with this priceless knowledge. Get ready to make memories that will last a lifetime by packing your luggage, donning your explorer's hat, and setting out. Cheers to your journey!

Conclusion

Resources

1. Skyscanner: Use the top flight search engine to find cheap flights and unearth undiscovered vacation gems.
2. Hostelworld: Thanks to their user-friendly layout, you may quickly choose the appropriate hostel lodging from the broadest selection accessible.
3. Booking.com: Securing great discounts on affordable lodging with a wide variety of possibilities.
4. Get Your Guide: Access an extensive selection of city tours and excursions worldwide, conveniently in one location, to streamline your holiday planning.
5. LifeStraw: Keep yourself hydrated during your travel by ensuring access to clean drinking water while on the go with their reusable bottles that have built-in filters.
6. SafetyWing: Enjoy peace of mind throughout your long-term or digital nomad travels with insurance plans created just for you, giving convenience and price.

7. Unbound Merino: Their travel clothing line offers breathable, long-lasting, and simple-to-maintain clothing that is ideal for your trips. Travel light and feel comfortable.

Looking Back at the Loire Valley's Beauty and Charm

It's difficult to resist being overcome by this French wonderland's breathtaking beauty and unmistakable charm as we near the conclusion of our adventure through the enthralling Loire Valley. The Loire Valley is a place that captures the heart and makes an enduring impression on the soul, from the towering châteaux that appear to have emerged from the pages of a fairy tale to the lovely vineyards that cover the undulating hills.

The Loire Valley is a place where extraordinary opportunities abound. Wander through the picturesque lanes of little towns where the aroma of freshly made bread mixes with the whispers of legends from centuries past. Enjoy the stunning view that varies with each pedal stroke as you lazily pedal along the Loire River on a bicycle. Enjoy delicious food while tasting the flavors of locally sourced foods and regional delicacies that will leave you wanting more.

Every moment in the Loire Valley offers the chance to make memories that you'll cherish long after you've left. Whether you're taking in the magnificence of Château de Chambord, strolling through Villandry's immaculate gardens, or enjoying a superb wine as the sun sets over the vineyards, each encounter is a gift to be treasured.

Carry the Loire Valley's beauty, charm, and remarkable experiences with you as you say goodbye to this lovely region. Let it motivate you to seek out new experiences, respect many cultures, and carry on discovering the treasures the world has to offer. Cheers to your journey!

Planning your itinerary

Let's start preparing for that trip!

Should you change your mind, fill in with a pencil.

Little bit of advice:
Mix & match: Like a delicious buffet, the Loire Valley has something to offer everyone, from captivating castle tours and wine tastings to discovering rich culture and beautiful settings. Get ready to construct a varied schedule that will leave you wanting more by donning your adventurous spirit.

Think about the Distance and Time: My fellow travelers, it's crucial to make prudent plans given the size of the Loire Valley. To avoid feeling hurried, take into account travel times and distances between locations. Allow yourself plenty of time to thoroughly appreciate each spectacular moment and take in the natural splendor that is all around you. Keep in mind that the key to fully appreciating this wonderful place is to move slowly and steadily.

Use Local Wisdom: Consult the Locals When in Doubt! They are the key to the lesser-known gems and undiscovered treasures of their cherished Loire Valley. Engage in cordial dialogue with the hospitable people and allow their firsthand expertise to guide your adventure. The locals will direct you towards amazing experiences, whether it's a secluded garden or a little village off the beaten route.

Prepare to savor the Loire Valley's rich tapestry, my fellow travelers. Make your own itinerary by mixing and matching the stunning castles, wine tastings, cultural experiences, and scenic scenery. Never forget to take time and distance into account, ask the locals for guidance, and set out on a journey that will fill your heart with memories that will last a lifetime. Allow the Loire Valley to enthrall your senses and produce a trip that is genuinely extraordinary.

In order to fully experience the Loire Valley region and visit the well-known châteaux without being too worn out, two or three days are sufficient1. However, it is advised to stay at least three full days in the Loire Valley, ideally five or six.

Flight Details

	Date	Airline	Arrival Time	Destination	Gate

Car Rentals

Date	Time	Location	Company

Accommodation

Check in Date	Name	Location	Room	Check out Date

Day 1

Time duration	Destination
Morning ___ to ___ hrs\min	
Breakfast ___ to ___ hrs\min	
Afternoon ___ to ___ hrs\min	
Lunch ___ to ___ hrs\min	
Evening ___ to ___ hrs\min	
Dinner ___ to ___ hrs\min	
Transport ___ to ___ hrs\min	

Day 2

Time duration	Destination
Morning ___ to ___ hrs\min	
Breakfast ___ to ___ hrs\min	
Afternoon ___ to ___ hrs\min	
Lunch ___ to ___ hrs\min	
Evening ___ to ___ hrs\min	
Dinner ___ to ___ hrs\min	
Transport ___ to ___ hrs\min	

Day 3

Time duration	Destination
Morning ___ to ___ hrs\min	
Breakfast ___ to ___ hrs\min	
Afternoon ___ to ___ hrs\min	
Lunch ___ to ___ hrs\min	
Evening ___ to ___ hrs\min	
Dinner ___ to ___ hrs\min	
Transport ___ to ___ hrs\min	

Day 4

Time duration	Destination
Morning ___ to ___ hrs\min	
Breakfast ___ to ___ hrs\min	
Afternoon ___ to ___ hrs\min	
Lunch ___ to ___ hrs\min	
Evening ___ to ___ hrs\min	
Dinner ___ to ___ hrs\min	
Transport ___ to ___ hrs\min	

Day 5

Time duration	Destination
Morning ___ to ___ hrs\min	
Breakfast ___ to ___ hrs\min	
Afternoon ___ to ___ hrs\min	
Lunch ___ to ___ hrs\min	
Evening ___ to ___ hrs\min	
Dinner ___ to ___ hrs\min	
Transport ___ to ___ hrs\min	

Day 6

Time duration	Destination
Morning ___ to ___ hrs\min	
Breakfast ___ to ___ hrs\min	
Afternoon ___ to ___ hrs\min	
Lunch ___ to ___ hrs\min	
Evening ___ to ___ hrs\min	
Dinner ___ to ___ hrs\min	
Transport ___ to ___ hrs\min	

Day 7

Time duration	Destination
Morning ___ to ___ hrs\min	
Breakfast ___ to ___ hrs\min	
Afternoon ___ to ___ hrs\min	
Lunch ___ to ___ hrs\min	
Evening ___ to ___ hrs\min	
Dinner ___ to ___ hrs\min	
Transport ___ to ___ hrs\min	

Returning Flight

	Date	Airline	Arrival Time	Destination	Gate

Printed in Great Britain
by Amazon

26155143R10057